Living in a Village

in a

Richard Spilsbury

www.heinemannlibrary.co.uk

Visit our website to find out more information about Heinemann Library books.

To order:

☎ Phone +44 (0) 1865 888066

🖷 Fax +44 (0) 1865 314091

🖳 Visit www.heinemannlibrary.co.uk

Edited by Charlotte Guillain and
  Catherine Veitch
Designed by Joanna Hinton-Malivoire
Original illustrations © Capstone Global Library
Illustrated by Joanna Hinton-Malivoire
Picture research by Elizabeth Alexander and
  Fiona Orbell
Originated by Dot Gradations Ltd
Printed in China by South China Printing Company Ltd

ISBN 978 0 431020 85 3 (hardback)
14 13 12 11 10
10 9 8 7 6 5 4 3 2 1

British Library Cataloguing in Publication Data
Spilsbury, Richard
Living in a village. – (Our local area)
10.9'1734-dc22
A full catalogue record for this book is available from the British Library.

Acknowledgements
We would like to thank the following for permission to reproduce photographs: Alamy pp. **7** (© John Morrison), **18** (© Robert Harding Picture Library Ltd.), **20** (© EKP); © Capstone Global Library pp. **6**, **8**, **9**, **10**, **11** & **12** (Tudor Photography); Collections pp. **15** (Nigel Haggerty), **17** (David M. Hughes); Corbis pp. **4** & **5** (©Richard Klune), **13** (© Paul Thompson); Getty Images p. **16** (Brand New Images); Panos Pictures p. **19** (Jean Leo Dugast); Pictures of Britain p. **14** (©Michael Boulton).

Cover photograph of early morning at Castle Combe village reproduced with permission of Corbis (© Peter Adams).

We would like to thank Rachel Bowles for her invaluable help in the preparation of this book.

Every effort has been made to contact copyright holders of material reproduced in this book. Any omissions will be rectified in subsequent printings if notice is given to the publisher.

All the Internet addresses (URLs) given in this book were valid at the time of going to press. However, due to the dynamic nature of the Internet, some addresses may have changed, or sites may have changed or ceased to exist since publication. While the author and publisher regret any inconvenience this may cause readers, no responsibility for any such changes can be accepted by either the author or the publisher.

Contents

Any words appearing in the text in bold, **like this**, are explained in the glossary.

What is a village?

A village is a small type of **settlement**. Villages are usually smaller than towns, and are much smaller than cities. There may be fewer than 100 people, say five to thirty families, living in an average village. However, some large villages have several hundred people living in them.

This village is surrounded by countryside with fields and woods.

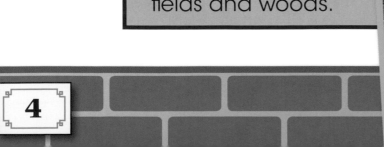

Villages are usually in the countryside.
The buildings are close together and
surrounded by fields and farmland.
Many villages are near a stream or river.
In the past, people built villages here
so they could get water.

Village buildings

Most of the buildings in a village are different types of homes. There may be old **cottages** and groups of new houses. In many villages there is also a village hall, a church, a pub, and a small park or open field where children can play. Think of three ways in which this is like where you live.

What do you think the buildings and open spaces in this village are for?

Try making a model or map of an imaginary village with a shop like this.

Larger villages may have several small shops, such as a **grocery**, a **butcher's shop**, and a post office. Small villages and smaller **settlements** called **hamlets** have no shop at all. Many villages have one shop that sells a mix of things, like newspapers, bread, and other food.

Village transport

Many villages are so small that people can walk from one end to the other. If a village is not too hilly, people may cycle around. Villagers travel by bus or car to other villages, to nearby towns or to the nearest city. They go there to shop, to work, or to have fun.

Buses do not stop in villages many times each day, so villagers need to check the bus timetable carefully.

Lorries and vans may deliver oil for heating homes, or shopping that people order on the Internet. A fish and chip van may come to sell people a takeaway meal.

This is a library van and it is full of books. The library van travels to different villages on different days. The librarian lends books to the people who live in the villages.

Village days

Often people work in the village where they live. Farmers work in the fields and shopkeepers work in the shops. Other villagers have craft studios where they make furniture or pots, or paint pictures. Some people work at home, for example writing books, or mending computers.

If you owned a village shop, what things would you sell?

A village can be quiet and empty in the day. Children may go by bus or car to a school in a nearby town. Many adults leave the village to go shopping, or to work in a town or city nearby. When most people are not in a village during the day, it is often called a **commuter** village.

These village children are driven to and from a school in town each day.

In the past

What clues about the past can you find in your local area? This house is called the Old Bakehouse because it was where people made bread to sell to villagers in the past. Other words on village signs that tell us about the past are "smithy" and "cobbler". What do they mean?

Walk around your local area and take photos or draw pictures of places that remind you how people used to live.

The platform where people once got on and off trains now has tables and chairs on it.

The tearoom in the photograph used to be the waiting room and platform of a village railway station. The station closed because people started to get around by car more than by train.

Village fun

At the weekend, many villagers enjoy the countryside. They may fly kites, walk their dogs, ride their bikes or horses, or just go for a walk. Some villagers go to a cinema, theatre, or swimming pool in a town or city nearby.

People ride ponies to explore their local area.

Many village schools have a
summer **fete** to raise money.

Sometimes, everyone in the village gets
together. They may meet in the village
hall for a quiz or party. In summer, there is
often a summer fair with **stalls**, music, and
homemade cakes.

Village visitors

People come back to the village to visit their relatives at weekends and during holidays.

Some young people leave their village when they grow up. They move to a city to study, or to find a job, or a house to live in.

People from towns and cities like to visit villages, too. They come to walk or play in the countryside around the village. They eat dinner in the village pub. Some villages have cafés and gift shops for visitors.

Why do you think people like to walk through villages?

World villages

There are villages all over the world. People live in villages in different kinds of countryside. There are villages in tall forests, on faraway **islands**, up high mountains, in the middle of vast **grasslands**, and out by desert **oases**.

To visit this mountain village in Nepal, you have to climb a long way, or fly there in a plane.

People often build their village homes from materials they find nearby. Many village homes in the United Kingdom and the rest of the world are made of mud, stone, or wood. Villagers make roofs from overlapping stone, layers of long leaves, **wood shingles**, or even grasses.

In this village in Borneo, lots of families live together in the same building. In what ways is this village different to where you live?

Village changes

Life in a village can change. When more people move into a village to live, there are usually more cars. This makes village roads busy and more dangerous.

A village gets bigger when people build new houses there.

Theo's class is worried about the traffic since their village grew. They made a model of the village showing their homes and the places they need to go, such as the local school. They discussed ways to slow traffic down. Where would you put traffic lights or a **pedestrian crossing** where you live to make it safer to cross roads?

Theo's class made a list saying what they like and dislike about village changes.

LIKES

More houses means more people to play with

More houses means we may get a new shop

More people means we may get more buses each day

People might start businesses and give villagers jobs

DISLIKES

More people drive so there is more traffic

More people drop more litter

More people make more noise

Where in the village?

This is a village map. Imagine you walk along the road from South Farm to a friend's house in New Estate at the top of the village. What would you pass along the way? Describe your journey to someone new to the village.

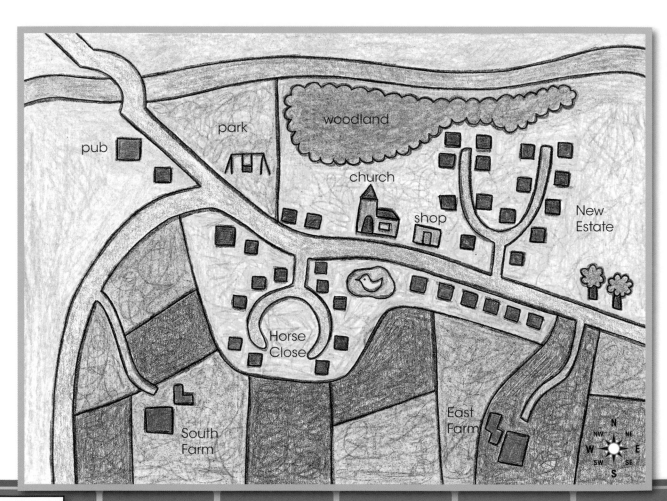

Glossary

commuter person who travels regularly between home and work

cottage small type of house

butcher's shop shop where people prepare and sell meat

fete special outdoor event with stalls and games, to raise money – perhaps for a school or a church

grasslands large area covered in grass

grocery shop selling food and different supplies for houses

hamlet tiny settlement of just a few similar houses in the countryside

island area of land surrounded by water

oases places in a desert with a spring or well of water. They are rich in plant life for food and animals.

pedestrian crossing road crossing for people on foot

settlement place where people have arrived and set up homes

stall table or counter used by someone selling goods

wood shingles thin, rectangular pieces of wood that are used to make roofs

Index

Find out more

Books to read

Islamic Village Stories (Six Paperback Book Set), Lugman Nagy
(Goodword Books, 2003)

Websites

Primary Global Eye – On Camera
www.globaleye.org.uk/primary_spring03/oncamera/index.html
This website includes photos of some of the different homes in villages
and other settlements where people live around the world.